Sea Trails

Poems and 1977 Passage Notes

By Pris Campbell

ISBN 978-1-929878-02-4

First edition

Lummox Press
PO Box 5301
San Pedro, CA 90733
www.lummoxpress.com

Printed in the United States of America

Acknowledgements: *Original Sin* was published in **Wild Goose Review,** *Streaking* was in **Empowerment4Women** and *Plymouth* was in **Not Your Bitch** at Outside Writers

Special thanks go to Carter Monroe, Scott Owens and Margie Stevenson for reading the collection and making helpful suggestions.

Sea Trails

How It Began

This 1977 trip was the fulfillment of a dream that the man I will only refer to as R and I had, individually. Together, we decided to make it reality. We lived in a commune in Boston where expenses were low, but we still put ourselves on a strict budget for two years. No frills allowed. My income was the one high enough to qualify for a boat loan after we discovered the boat that was to become Little Adventure. In the late seventies, women still couldn't be granted a loan unless a husband or financially responsible male co-signed. I went to the bank manager after being turned down by the assistants. He turned out to be a sailor, himself, broke the rules and gave me the loan. For that, I'm grateful. I'm also grateful that such limitations no longer exist for women.

Over the next two years we took Power Squadron courses on everything from what knot fits what occasion to advanced navigation to sail to engine maintenance. We practiced sail maneuvers and man overboard drills as part of our preparation. Our savings were meant to last for a year. They came mostly from my salary while R paid off an old college loan.

I also paid health insurance for a year in advance for us both at a time when that was completely affordable for people who weren't wealthy.

Our relationship, however, was dying as the time neared for us to go, but the trip had taken on a life of its own. R's anger over my job success compared to his was a barbed wire for me to deal with. His eye was beginning to rove, too. I wanted this trip, though, and wasn't out of love yet. Maybe I hoped the trip would bring back what we'd lost. We gave notice in our jobs, said our good-byes and left.

Was it crazy? Yes, in terms of our deteriorating relationship. No, in terms of what was to become one of the most meaningful adventures of my lifetime.

>>Log Entry—
Little Adventure: Fitting out the boat. June 1977

Little Adventure is a Tanzer 22 fin keel sailboat, purchased second-hand in Marion, MA, in late 1974. No standing head room in the cabin. She came with two regular jibs (Genoa for light winds and standard size), one small storm jib made of thick canvass, and a compass. R and I add a depth sounder, odometer, ship to shore radio and, before our trip, a second five gallon gas tank and homemade spinnaker. We purchase an Avon to serve as combination dinghy and life raft to replace the fiberglass dinghy we owned the first two years. A supply of paperback books are stored on a shelf in the main cabin where one quarterberth cushion slides back and a pop-up table comes up for meals and for chart space for course plotting.

As the trip's leave date nears, jeans and tee shirts are packed into two duffel bags and warmer clothes combined into a third, smaller duffel bag. Nets in the V-berth hold our toiletries. Wet gear hangs from a hook. Canned goods are stored in plastic bins beneath the quarter berths. Potatoes and onions hang from a net in the cabin. Block ice goes into a small front-opening ice chest built into the boat below the stove and sink. We have no hanging locker, no head. A porta potty will have to do. Our cat Monster's litter box sits under the lip of the V-berth where we'll sleep. A two-burner alcohol stove is mounted next to a sink too small to do dishes in. A bucket will do for that. Our goal is to make it to Florida, then across the Gulf Stream and down the Abacos, possibly ending up in New Orleans, a city we feel will be similar in spirit to Boston.

Sea Trails

I must go down to the sea again…
—John Masefield

I board the tiny sloop that has carried me
twice to Maine with its deep
silent harbors and moaning buoys.
I'm ensnared, trapped by increasing
longings to ride that magic carpet
into places different from my own
narrow world of nine to five rewind.
Saltwater rises through my body,
is transformed through its heat
into golden mist. I expand
without Alice's cookies,
become a gull dropping clams
on the rocks to crack them,
a molting lobster, a leaping dolphin,
a man watching the sky from a deserted dock.
The sea is my cradle and it rocks me,
lulling me into new ways of seeing.
My arms unfurl into sails.
I let the wind take me.

>>Log Entry—

July 4-6,1977. Home anchorage, Hull, MA to Plymouth Harbor

June winds have finally settled enough to make the trip possible. At 7 p.m., R rows back to the boat with two friends for a moonlight sail, after bringing in the last of our supplies. The skies have cleared and it's warm. The horizon turns red as we look at the Boston skyline for the last time. While we cook supper afterwards, two commune mates arrive with their Irish setter, happy to be reunited with Monster. All of us manage to crowd aboard to say final good-byes. We'll miss Boston. We'll miss good friends.

July 6: High winds kept us from leaving Hull yesterday, so today we head out of Hull Bay towards Harding Ledge. We fly the spinnaker in the light winds, making between 3 to 4 knots speed, then motor through the winding entrance to Plymouth Harbor where we moor next to the Mayflower, within sight of Plymouth Rock. Other boats near us are from Pennsylvania and New Jersey. The Cape Cod Canal is next. Our journey has begun.

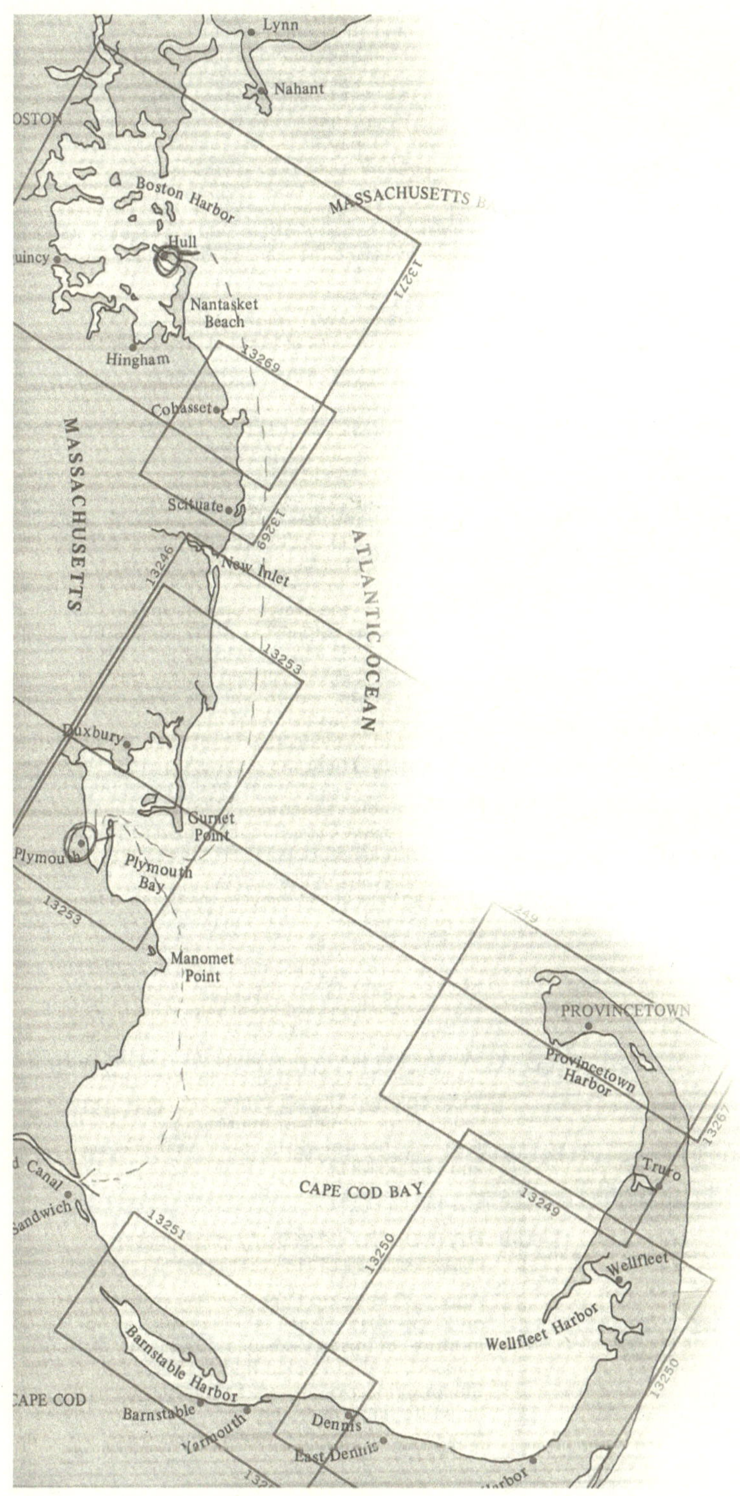
Lynn
Nahant
BOSTON
Boston Harbor
MASSACHUSETTS BAY
Hull
Quincy
Nantasket Beach
13271
Hingham
13269
Cohasset
MASSACHUSETTS
Scituate
13269
13246
New Inlet
ATLANTIC OCEAN
13253
Duxbury
Gurnet Point
Plymouth
Plymouth Bay
13253
Manomet Point
PROVINCETOWN
Provincetown Harbor
13267
Truro
Canal
Sandwich
CAPE COD BAY
13249
13251
13250
Wellfleet
Wellfleet Harbor
Barnstable Harbor
13250
CAPE COD
Barnstable
Yarmouth
Dennis
East Dennis

Spells

We see them from our boat,
these men and women dressed up
in Pilgrim clothes, as if Plymouth
is the new Brigadoon reincarnated
daily around a fake rock.
Had I been a real Pilgrim
I would've run off with a handsome
Medicine Man, slept on rabbit fur.
I would've warned my Medicine man
husband about the carnage already
brewing on the easterly winds.
I would've asked him to cast spells
upon all the birds in the forest
so their songs would bring peace
to land-greedy white men with guns
and Indians painting themselves
black and orange beside rising war fires.
Village and woods would be filled
with children of all colors,
beads clattering around their necks,
bellies filled with porridge.
I try to smoke the peace pipe with my lover,
one quarter Indian, himself,
but I never ran off with the Medicine Man
and the birds never sang their magic.
He slashes my throat with a word
and I bleed onto the deck until our boat
is drenched with the color of sunset.

Why I call him my Lover

He's not my mate.
Not my husband, either.
I don't think of him
as my partner.
He's not sweetie, hon,
darlin', or luv.
I no longer use his given
name except when calling him.
We create what seems like love
in the V-berth each evening
and, sometimes, for a sail
flutter, it is again.
That and the boat
are our only tether.
The thread between us
is bound to break
by journey's end.
I fear my fall back to earth
will be harder than his.

I breathe in the sea air,
deny craters left
by growing anger.
The sky is golden.
The sea creates its own
rhythm beneath me.
Night falls and he kisses me.

Once Upon a Time

It wasn't always like this;
boxing gloves on,
barbed-wire fences raised.
We could melt windows,
set trees on fire, make stars
fall from a frozen sky.
He was my mainsail.
I was his boat,
bearing him to wild new shores.
We drank from the same cup,
shared passion like fine wine
until our bodies moved as the tide does,
finding its way home to the moon again.

Maneuvers at Sea

Tacking or ***coming about*** *is the maneuver by which a sailing vessel turns its bow through the wind so that the wind changes from one side to the other. For example, if a vessel is sailing on a starboard tack (with the wind to starboard) and tacks, it will end up on a port tack, with the wind to port.* ***Tacking is distinct from jibing where the ship's stern passes through the wind.***

Reversals

I hold this picture...
us, coming west through
the Cape Cod Canal
in our proud new boat--not east,
a different couple then,
sunlight teasing our hair,
sky etching us blue into its memory.
Us, bringing Little Adventure home
to Hull, hands touching, cheeks flushed.

Now, tide turned, the sunshine grows weary;
sky fades to pale.
We head toward rising plovers
and racing clouds, clanking halyards
and fluttering sails, sea air swelling our lungs.
Unknown harbors wait to embrace us,
to cast roses upon hope that what
has been lost can still find fresh breath.

A jibe or gybe *is a maneuver where a sailing vessel turns its stern through the wind, such that the wind direction changes from one side of the boat to the other. The mainsail will cross the center of the boat while the jib (forward sail) is pulled to the other side of the boat.*

A more complicated maneuver involves letting anger sail past, finding beauty around you when the close-up ugly threatens to intrude.

Rebirth

Tiller clutched between knees for steering,
crouched over, eyes scanning the horizon,
I nudge our bow towards the outreached boom.
When the wind finally loosens its grip,
I pull the line fast, hand over hand.
My legs become coils, balancing me
as we slide into the trough.
Today's wind turns stronger than a trumpet's wail,
and the boom pauses mid-ship, as if to warn me,
crosses over, until our mainsail strains white
against blue again. A Paul Newman sky.
The head of our little boat is crowning
into Newman's eyes.
I've birthed her hundreds of times
just as she's birthed me,
but each time is a new time.
Umbilical cut, we move towards the open sea.

>>Log Entry—
July10-16 Cuttyhunk Harbor, through Martha's Vineyard, to Nantucket Island

We sail to Cuttyhunk, the first of the Vineyard islands, from Quissett Harbor. The passage to the inner harbor is narrow. At low tide there's no room for small boat and ferry to pass. The ferry is the only source of groceries and mail to the island. It also is the only way to get to the island without a small boat. Cuttyhunk is small and quiet. The post office is in someone's home. The grocery store is a small building behind someone else's home. We pay eight dollars for a supply of groceries and are surprised to see cars since the ferry isn't a large one. After exploring the island, we spend two days watching boats come in from as far away as San Francisco and rowing onshore again to admire the long hilly stretches of fields and woods.

July 14: We leave Cuttyhunk for Vineyard Haven. Out of land's shelter, the seas build to six feet and we're tossed about in the swells. The tiller is hard to hold steady. By late morning, the winds die and the seas begin to calm. This portion of the Vineyard is hilly and green with sandy cliffs along the ocean. Fancy homes dot the shoreline. At 1400 hours we round the buoy that marks shoaling out from Vineyard Haven and follow the red and green channel markers into the small harbor. We spend fifteen dollars for groceries, block ice and a bottle of scotch. That evening, we splurge by eating out at an inexpensive pub near the harbor.

July 15: *We hoist anchor at 0720. Slight chance of rain predicted. We're pushed off course by the winds and tide. Corrected. Back on course. At 1015 we round black can '21', out of sight of land now in all directions due to the distance between islands and patches of fog. We're a little nervous, hope we haven't been thrown off of our dead reckoning course for Nantucket. At 1220, to our relief, we close in on the buoy that marks our final six mile stretch. Hazy land appears in the distance. At 1451 we enter Nantucket harbor and drop anchor. We're held here until the 27th by gale force winds and small craft advisories throughout the Vineyard.*

Unsafe Harbors

Out of the horseshoe that is Cuttyhunk,
anchor hauled from Vineyard Haven,
where a hopeful fan mistakes me for Joni Mitchell,
past where John Kennedy, Jr. is to later plunge
to his death, we reach Nantucket, cobblestoned home
to the tourists, small boaters and the wealthy.
A distant dot on the chart;
miss it and you're enroute to England.
It's my birthday and the clanking halyards,
the ricky-tick shops become my present,
my 'happy birthday to you', my respite
from my lover's glares, his increasing nips at my ankles.
I glow, even in this heartless town where
hand painted rocks go for hundreds of bucks
and no homeless sit on the cobblestone begging for cash.
Its disturbing beauty washes over me,
like the long warm showers at the marina,
so when the winds rise later,
sneaking up through that vulnerable spot
in the anchorage I'm reminded that
there are no safe harbors, no havens.
We run the motor all night, ease the strain
on the groaning anchor rode, watch
skeletons of boats slip past our starboard
and port sides, hope we won't be hit,
dragged back in this black night along with them.
Daybreak brings scratched, tangled and beached boats.
but our shadow passes, unscathed,
across the morning water.

Small Craft Advisories

We plot our escape past the angry nor'easter
pummeling the Vineyard with fifty knot punches.
For seven days and seven nights now,
we've cowered in this tense harbor.
Birds take shelter in bent trees.
The sun hides its face in shame.
Small dogs tuck tails between legs, run inland.
Double reefed, we nose out Nantucket's
razor rock jetty, hands bleeding fright.
Are you crazy, megaphones a Mack Truck,
disguised as a battened-down fishing boat.
The Coast Guard roars by, casting its surf.
Reversing direction, Little Adventure heels hard,
struggles back up against the seething waves.
I teeter below into the blend of UFO dishes,
sliding duffels, flying forks, try to tuck things away.
Monster leaps to my lap, gouges claws into knees
in this fear-bond between shaking fur, human skin.
Re-anchored, we clean and collapse.
Our boat peels back her hull, reveals inner scars.
My heart laid open, she already knows mine.

>>Log Entry—
July 27-29 Nantucket to Newport, via Cuttyhunk

We haul anchor at 0810 for the long 45 mile run to Cuttyhunk, as a stopover to our next stop. Newport, Rhode Island. We don't go ashore on this stopover. Instead, we read and go to sleep early.

July 28: *We haul anchor to begin our sail at 0900 on a sunny day with light winds from the west. At 1530 we round the final bend to Newport harbor. The first anchorage area is calm but isn't close enough to row to the city docks. Exhausted, we drop anchor, anyway and overnight here.*

July 29-August 1: *At 0800 we re-anchor closer in to the city docks, where we are surrounded by sailboats from all over the country and some from overseas. A small motorboat comes around, run by two gals, selling doughnuts, newspapers, taking in trash for a .75 cents a bag and even your laundry. Twenty-five pounds of block ice costs a dollar plus 1.50 delivery fee. This service is a first! We go to shore where we shower, grocery shop, do our own laundry, and explore the city. It's America's Cup trials period and time for the Newport to Bermuda race, so Newport is packed with sailors. One evening we visit with an Australian reporter and his wife, here to cover the Cups race. We stay until August 1, then sail on down the coast to Galilee.*

Newport Mayhem

Memories of navy years here with my first husband
worm their way into uncertain spaces
between new ones I'm creating. I ghost-walk
docks I walked many times with my ex,
tell him the earth skidded sideways when we split,
speak of old friends, days at Pearl Harbor,
forget he lost the urge to plumb the mystery
I was when we were wed.

Nostalgia gradually lifts.
We stuff ourselves at Salas',
guzzle too many banana daiquiris.
Tipsy, we wander through the mayhem
of Newport during race week.

The birdlike 12 meters, keels wrapped for secrecy,
tremble with excitement, strain at their lines.
Past them, larger sailboats with winches
wide as a fat man's thigh and lines nested
over busy decks, await their sprint for Bermuda.

Parties spill onto the docks.
Excitement crackles like flash lightning.

I've already become part gypsy, but I'm glad
my palm doesn't tell me the Navy base will
close later, enlisted men will no longer
wander the town, the Cup will leave Newport
and malls will spring up like weeds along the harbor,

displacing aging nooks where the Black Pearl
still serves the best clam chowder in town.
I'm glad to sit on Little Adventure
under the darkening plum colored sky, feeling
every fresh second merge with my heartbeat
until my chest splits wide open to the glory of now.

Definitions

line: *A rope becomes a line when attached to a boat. It becomes a rope again when completely detached and removed from the boat.*

rode: *Name used specifically for line tied to the anchor.*

scope: *The amount of anchor rode let out in an anchorage. The deeper the water and the more severe the weather the more rode you will put out. For recreational boaters you should have out five to eight times the depth of the water plus the distance from the water to where the anchor will attach to the bow. You put out more for overnight or in stormy conditions, less for temporary day anchoring in calm waters.*

anchor rode: *Line, chain or a combination of both. The whole system of gear including anchor, rode, shackles etc. is called ground tackle.*

Dead Reckoning

Dead reckoning involves estimating one's current position based upon a previously determined position, or fix, and advancing that position forward on a chart, based upon known speed, elapsed time, and course. There are no buoys or landmarks to go by, only this course, which must be adjusted along the way as currents, boat speed and winds change.

Galilee

He calls himself Harpoon Louis, rows
to our boat from a once beautiful
but time-betrayed wooden sloop.
The Wayward Wind can still be made out
in faded letters on its stern.
Sad, torn sails, despairing shrouds,
jilted charts with footprints
all over them litter the cockpit.
He's been trying to return home
to Long Island each fall now, he tells us.
The Coast Guard always tows him back in.
He eats from the dumpsters, plentiful
behind the many seafood restaurants
filling this commercial seaport town,
a town where Christ, himself, could
break bread and visitors would be too stuffed
with fresh fish and fritters to notice.
I wonder where Louis sleeps when frost
kisses the air, when snow rests its head
against his cold cabin.
I wonder if his skeleton will someday
be found by a fisherman, hand still on the tiller,
Long Island chart at his feet, fish
circling his keel in mourning.

>>Log Entry—
August 5

August 5: We leave Galilee for Block Island, planning to just overnight in the harbor but not go ashore. 'Doc', on a 37 foot Irwin, whom we met in Newport is there so we spend part of the evening visiting with him on his boat. "Doc' is a 66 year old twice-widowed retired physician. He's been sailing for three years and plans to 'go on as long as he can'.

We arrived just before fog set in and the harbor entrance disappeared. We leave the following morning for Stonington Harbor, CT, marking the very beginning of our trip through Long Island Sound. Thick fog follows us all of the way and we rely on dead reckoning to find our jetty. One-fourth of a mile offshore we finally see land and the jetty is directly in front of us. Hooray! We see several boats we know, visit friends we met earlier now home onshore. We stay in the anchorage for two days.

Block Island

The anchorage is a basin
of relieved sailors
as the god-storm chasing us
wallops, then lifts.
Green hills emerge,
are trimmed back by the falling sun.
A shadow dressed in yellow raingear
walks to the soaked shore,
slides a dinghy higher, fades.
We sit on Karakal with Doc,
watch the water move through
a rainbow of sunset pinks,
speak of disgruntled seas,
worn-out sails.
Monster has ventured
onto the bow of our boat.
Her gold and white fur

is our flare when we row back.
A lock to my heart clicks open
and I want him to see me
again like he did when
my slippers were still shiny.
I touch his face.
His anger bubbles over.
Your hand is cold, he snaps.

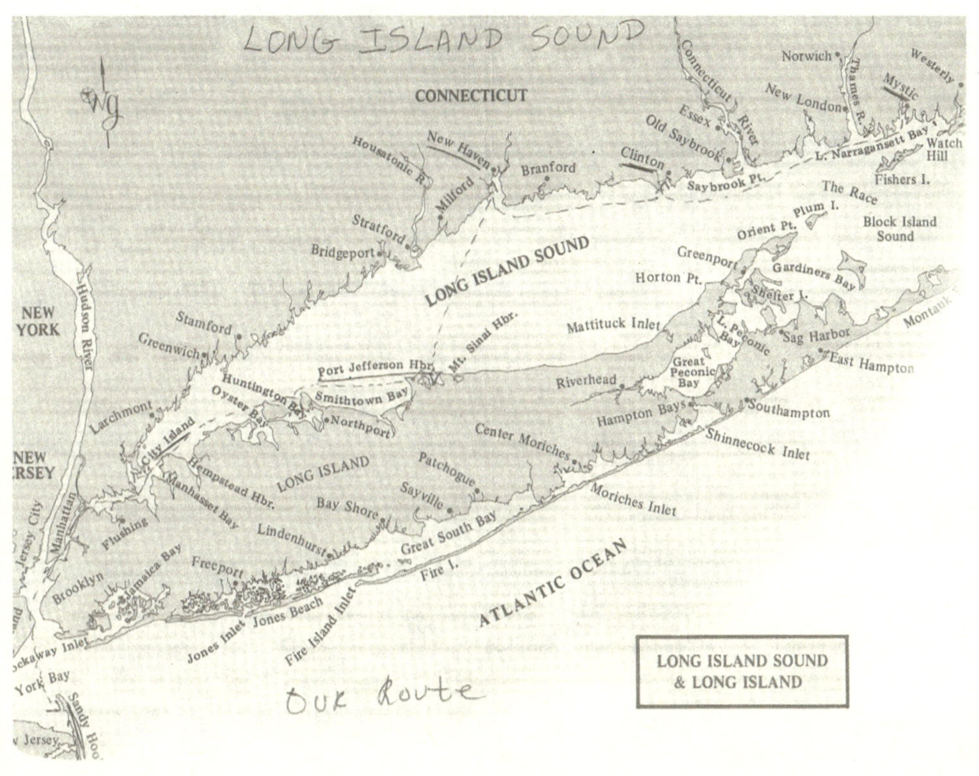

>>Log Entry—
August 7-15

The trip through Long Island Sound remains foggy. Sightings of shoreline on either the Connecticut side or the western New York side are rare until we near harbor. At Mystic, Connecticut we look up a couple we met in Nantucket. They rented the boat they had in Nantucket but are building their own for a later trip. They have us over for dinner, offer us warm showers and their car the following day to pick up supplies, then tour the Mystic Maritime Museum.

Port Jefferson, on the New York side is our other favorite harbor, with health food restaurants, antique stores and old, beautiful homes. We linger exploring land and shore, anchoring our second night out by a narrow edge of land that separates harbor from sound.

Fog

The sky is a woman
suppressing her tears.
I think that woman is me.

Fog II

Long Island Sound
is a ghost town.
Like Columbus,
we drift towards uncertain
horizons, ease up
to the moaning
Port Jefferson buoy,
head east, quaff
a full barrel of trust.

Sunrise. Nearing Atlantic City, N.J.

>>Log Entry—

August 16-18 City Island, Bronx to Sandy Hook, NJ

We grab a mooring at a City Island for five dollars since currents run strong now near the East River. We take the train into Manhattan one day, then buy supplies and attend our first movie of the trip…Star Wars, one recently out. We dread the East River run because of Hell's Gate, aptly named, a section mid-river that circles a small piece of land. Even at slack tide, the current can run four to five knots, difficult for our small motor to handle. For that brief period of time, the boat will almost be out of our control and we pray we don't meet a barge.

August 18: *We make it safely through Hell's Gate with our breath held as the boat rides with the current, almost out of control, then cruise on down the East River and out past the magnificent Statue of Liberty to anchor in Sandy Hook, NJ, overnight. Boats fill the harbor since it's a Sunday and I feel the excitement of Manhattan expanding out into the water. Tomorrow will be our run to Manisquan Inlet, one of three harbors along the entire Jersey coast deemed safe enough to enter without local knowledge.*

Parallel Currents

The Twin towers dress Manhattan's skyline
as the East River spits us
into New York harbor, past the Lady.
Manhattan still runs a parallel current
in my veins with the sea and I linger
at these crossroads between this city I love,
lived in briefly, and the quiet slosh
of harbor waters. I blow goodbye kisses
to Picasso's gaunt men at the MOMA,
to Debra Kerr and Cary Grant still racing
to show their love at the Empire State Building,
the imprint of song and word in the air
above Broadway and guitarists singing
for quarters at Washington Square.
We sail so close to the Lady I feel I can touch her
then suddenly we shimmer, become a dragonfly
buzzing across the harbor to Sandy Hook,
sea spray soaking our bow.

Streaking

I want him inside me before weighing anchor,
certain Neptune will rise, enraged and hungry,
out of those black Jersey seas
to swallow us whole on this long night run
from Manisquan to Atlantic City.
I pull him into me hard--wild animals rutting
in this coffin-like cabin, feet kicking *yes*
to the seawater slosh outside.

We stopped making love months ago.
Now we just use each other's bodies
to unleash our fears and occasionally
discover buried treasure.

Red clouds bleed into a blind man's sky
when we finally set sail toward the wrecks
of Perkins and McAllister, to Dead Man's Reef,
where the bones of ancient mariners still rattle.
Surreal lights on the distant shore glow
as people come and go to K-Mart or McDonalds,
landlubbers with TV's in their dens,
kids stuck to their hands.

The cowardly moon blinks, drops out of sight
and Neptune appears in the rising winds.
He growls at his fleeing prey,
hurls spume at our boat,
denuded quickly to storm jib and hope.

Each time I clamp my lifeline to the wet
bucking deck I dream myself safe
in the arms of a man with thick legs and big hands,
a man who wants solid ground beneath his feet, but

I know that my siren sisters who called me
on other nights and who called me tonight,
won't easily release me, so strong
are the sea-borne threads between us.

I slip-climb back to my lover's lap,
let him fill me again as we
surf down the screaming seas,
arm braced beside his at the tiller.

I pretend he's an angel washed up over the railing,
his mouth rimmed with magic, his semen luminescent.

>>Log Entry—
Sept 12-13 Cohansey River in Delaware Bay to Chesapeake City in the C & D Canal connecting Delaware Bay to the Chesapeake Bay

We anchor at the Cohansey River after leaving the cut between Cape May, N.J. and the base of the Delaware Bay. Fore and aft anchors set because of the current. We see the Mary Margaret, a Grampian 32, that had been anchored close to us our last day at Cape May. Owners Dave and Margaret Rogers invite us over for a visit. He's retired military and she's a retired R.N. They've sold their Annapolis home and are heading south. Next morning we travel up the Delaware together. The chop is up and it's overcast. Huge freighters and powerboats race through the main channel, leaving our boat rocking. We travel most of the Delaware Bay far to the side of the main channel. When we enter the C & D Canal, the sun finally comes out.

The canal is crowded with boats, but the shoreline is beautiful. Tree lined and hilly. We anchor at Chesapeake City. The anchorage area has a three foot sand bar to avoid but the inside is deep and peaceful. The town looks deserted and rundown from the boat. We go ashore with Dave and Margaret and visit the museum that tells how the canal was created. Later, Dave hoists R up his mast in his boson's chair to fix something. I take photographs when Dave ties him up there for about 10 minutes as a joke. Tomorrow morning 's run is to the Bohemia River, only two hours away, at the upper mouth of the Chesapeake. We plan to anchor there with Dave and Margaret again before we spend the next three weeks explor-

ing the Bay. They'll return to Annapolis to say goodbye to friends again then work at the St Michaels' Maritime Museum for a short while before heading south again.

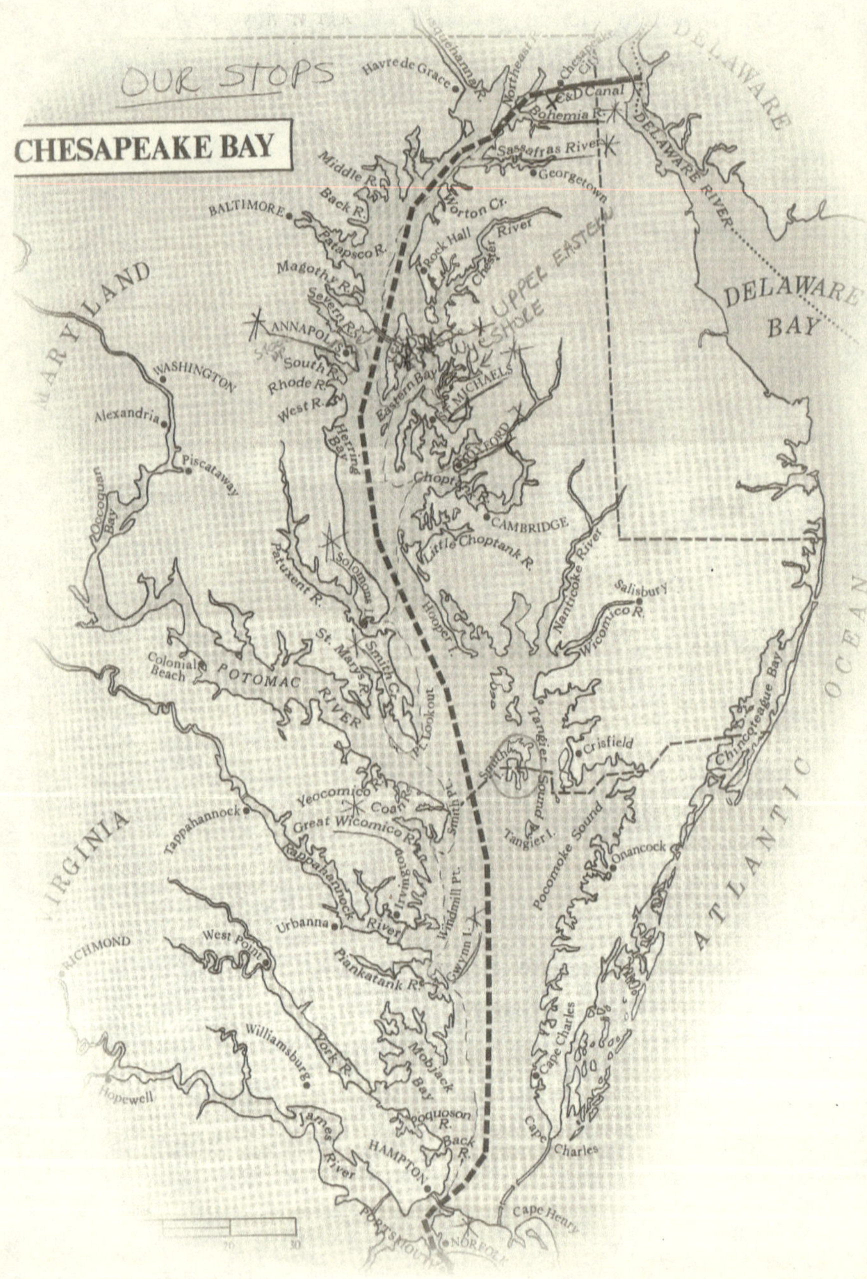
CHESAPEAKE BAY
OUR STOPS
UPPER EASTERN
WYE SHORE
MARYLAND
VIRGINIA
DELAWARE
DELAWARE BAY
DELAWARE RIVER
ATLANTIC OCEAN
Havre de Grace
Chesapeake City
C&D Canal
Bohemia R.
Sassafras River
Georgetown
Northeast R.
Middle R.
Back R.
BALTIMORE
Patapsco R.
Magothy R.
Severn R.
ANNAPOLIS
South R.
Rhode R.
West R.
Herring Bay
Worton Cr.
Rock Hall
Chester River
Eastern Bay
ST. MICHAELS
OXFORD
Choptank R.
CAMBRIDGE
Little Choptank R.
Nanticoke River
Salisbury
Wicomico R.
WASHINGTON
Alexandria
Piscataway
Occoquan Bay
Patuxent R.
Solomons I.
St. Marys R.
Smith Cr.
Colonial Beach
POTOMAC RIVER
Pt. Lookout
Hooper I.
Tangier Sound
Smith I.
Crisfield
Chincoteague Bay
Yeocomico
Coan R.
Great Wicomico R.
Smith Pt.
Tangier I.
Pocomoke Sound
Onancock
Tappahannock
Rappahannock River
Irvington
Windmill Pt.
Urbanna
Gwynn I.
West Point
RICHMOND
Piankatank R.
Williamsburg
York R.
Mobjack Bay
Poquoson R.
Hopewell
James River
HAMPTON
Back R.
Cape Charles
Cape Charles
Cape Henry
PORTSMOUTH
NORFOLK
20
30

Sea Speak

The Chesapeake opens beneath us,
a woman spreading her skirt wide
to greet the Atlantic, already throbbing
with September winds at her feet.
I learn to lay down a trot line,
haul hungry crabs to the surface, tossing
the lucky red-bellied females back.
I learn that fish gasp in upper Bay
pollution, that sea grass cries,
that watermen chug out at dawn past
clanging buoys and clearing mist
hoping to net their catch for the day.
I learn that heaven is right here
in these blue waters, the upside-down sky,
that the spirits of old sailors walk
on our bow at night, telling lost stories
about Tangier Isle, Shanks, Queens Ridge,
Piney Island. I learn how love
of the sea can rush right through you
with the wind, until your heart is translucent
with joy as intense as pain.

>>Log Entry —
Sept 15-17 St Michaels, MD Chesapeake Bay

We arrive in St Michaels for St Michaels' Week, with events such as the log canoe races, the old boat parade and exhibitions at the old Lighthouse. St Michaels is a small town, quiet and unsullied by tourism. Hope it will stay that way. We find Dave and Margaret here again, along with other boats we've seen and visited along the way.

It strikes us again that we've seen so many familiar faces over and over on our trip so far. We'd thought we would be traveling mostly alone but discover that there's a very real, moveable community of boaters going down the coast with us. The values are noticeably different from most places on land. We're often in situations when we could use a helping hand or offer one. Boaters say, 'Don't thank me. Just pass it on'. We find crop-haired military men sitting down at the chart table with long hairs. Neither would probably have passed the time of day on shore. It's an experience in communal living much more profound than the one I had found on shore.

Balancing Act

No keel to balance their tall masts
and broad sails on these smooth-bellied
log-canoe boats, the crew jams long planks
under the cockpit lip, switching sides at each tack.
They scramble to the end, their weight, ballast,
against the morning winds off St Michaels,
feet dangling over the green water.
I think of my own life,
balance so often uncertain,
my many tumbles into the drink.
No man has been my keel.
No man has climbed out over risky waters
to help hold me steady.
My men have been wind, always moving,
seeking fresh sails, new harbors to serenade.
His lips graze my neck.
I turn away, but my body betrays me.
My pulse quickens.
I no longer care if my tilt is too steep,
if my sails dunk low into the deep
silence of breath.

Crabbing

He still catches me
with the same old line,
the worn bait.
Just as I see light,
he nets me again.

How to lay a trot line for catching crabs

(An old crab fisherman we met at St Michaels taught us this method)

One bag of chunks of salt pork
One long line with the circumference of approximately a pencil. You have to be able to knot it easily around the salt pork
Net on a long pole.

With novices, this operation works best with two people.

Knot the salt pork onto the line at 6 foot intervals. Go to the stern of your boat and toss the line out a short distance, then continue with the rest of the line alongside the boat to the bow. Wait a few minutes. Slowly begin raising the line from the bow end. Have the net dipped slightly into the water just in front of the area you're lifting up. Crab will cling to the bait until they see surface light then let go. As soon as you spot the crab, set the net under it so that you catch it as it falls. Continue in the same fashion on down the line.

If you're lucky, crab on your plate for dinner!

>>Log Entry—
Sept 26 Smith Creek off the Potomac River

As we near the widening mouth of the Chesapeake, the winds grow stronger and the waves steeper, holding us in each port longer each time. We have three ports to go before we enter Newport News, buoy one of the Intracoastal Waterway at Norfolk. Plans to see Tangier Island are scuttled. We need to begin making our way south faster. After crabbing all day to catch only one crab a powerboat, The Nautigal II, enters the anchorage area, driven in, too, by the high waves. Powerboats rarely anchor out but go from marina to marina. They hail us and we dinghy over. A younger man, Eastern Airlines pilot, has flown up to help his friend bring his boat down to Florida. They tell us they are out of supplies, hoping originally to make the next harbor. We invite them over for dinner made from our one crab mixed with tomatoes and canned vegetables, sopped up with our remaining bread. All bellies are filled amply. Afterwards we row them back to their boat and sit up high in the captain's area. No lights can be seen on shore and the sky is beginning to clear. We watch the stars for an hour then row back to Little Adventure. When we arise at dawn the next morning they've already hauled anchor and gone.

Sept 27-Oct 3

We slowly make our way through higher seas down past Solomans, where we pick up mail sent there general delivery, then to Milford Haven where we stay Sept 30 to Oct4. Small craft advisories, steep seas and 25-35 knot winds hold us there. We meet Pete and Alberta from Turtle. They saved 12 years on a modest income to build Turtle and travel. They've sailed for three years around South America, Mexico and the Keys and are now living in a trailer onshore and working to go for seven more years on the boat. They 'home-schooled' their two daughters those three years. Both are now in regular high school for the year and doing well.

We've met two types of dropouts over the years. Most of the ones onshore who are healthy and dropping out to make a 'statement' have been dependent on Welfare or some type of government support. Seagoers drop out in a self-sufficient way, via savings and working along the way. They're more like the old Pioneers, going towards something, not away.

Little Red Riding Hood

The Big Bag Wolf huffs and puffs
near the mouth of the Chesapeake,
tries to blow our boat down.
We dash from harbor to harbor
on the southeastern rim
whenever he closes his eyes.
The harbors are paragons of calmness.
The Wolf hasn't found his way yet
into Solomans, Smith Creek, the Great
Wicomica River or Milford Haven.
We eat soft-shelled crabs, row ashore,
meet other refuges, crab, and sleep.
We try not to look like Little Red
Riding Hood with our red sheer stripe
and red-orange life jackets strapped
to our thudding chests whenever
we venture back out. I finally realize
that Jimmy Buffet's not going to sing
a Paradise song, the sea won't become
a magazine photo op, and we make our last run.
If the Wolf eats me I hope I'm not tasty.
I hope he spits me back out.

>>*Log Entry—*

October 4: *Pete and Alberta invite us for dinner and showers two nights, drive us for supplies. We regret telling them good-bye when the weather finally clears enough for our 78 mile run to Willoby Spit, just inside the Intracoastal Waterway. In a boat that makes 5 knots maximum speed, it's a long run. We catch the last rays of light as we finally drop our hook. The anchorage isn't well protected, so we spend a restless night checking to make sure the winds haven't caused us to slip.*

Big Red

Buoy number one
of the Intracoastal,
she bobs, bends,
clangs, preens.
Cameras click
as boaters pass by
capturing this special
moment, this mark.
Were she a person
she'd be Madonna
or Grace Slick,
decked out in red
and ready to party.

We putt past huge ships
at the Naval base.
Land cups us close
to port and starboard.
I watch Big Red recede
to our stern but
she doesn't miss us;
she's already entertaining
new guests.

>>Log Entry—
Oct 5-Oct 7 Newport News to Coinjack, next to Albemarle Sound

We're at at Newport News, Norfolk, mile one of the Intracoastal Waterway. Huge navy ships from the naval base in Norfolk line the Waterway as we head towards Coinjack, N.C. The ships are impressive, one after the other, towering over us along the dock. I've seen Pearl Harbor and Newport where the ships aren't so accessible to the public, so this is a surprise. We feel like a shrimp as we pass them.

At Coinjack we go though our first lock. The lock staff instruct us how to tie up on the port side of the lock with plenty of bumpers, then the water goes down and the lock on the other end opens. We tie up at Coinjack, waiting for the weather to clear to cross Albemarle Sound. The Chinese Junk we've seen is tied up there, too. The owners tell us they've lived aboard for nine years. She was a child psychologist.

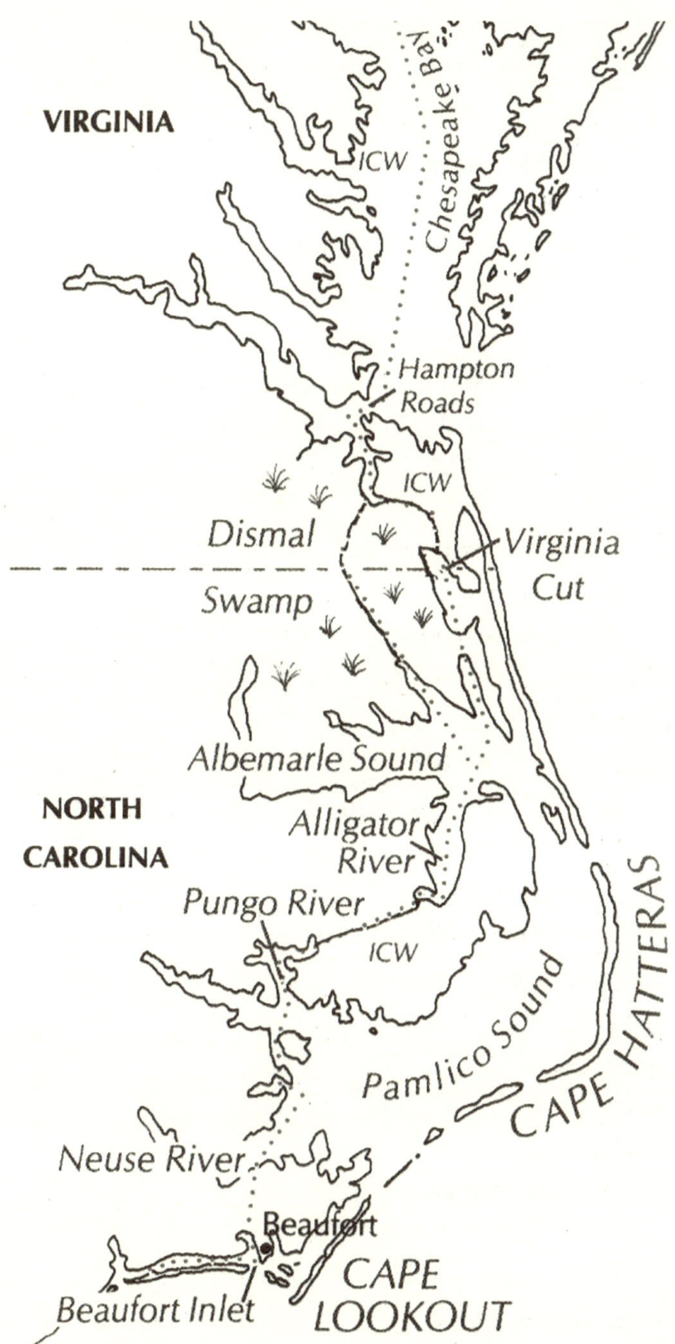
VIRGINIA
ICW
Chesapeake Bay
Hampton
Roads
ICW
Dismal
Virginia
Cut
Swamp
Albemarle Sound
NORTH
CAROLINA
Alligator
River
Pungo River
ICW
Pamlico Sound
CAPE HATTERAS
Neuse River
Beaufort
CAPE
LOOKOUT
Beaufort Inlet

The Great Escape

While we wait to cross
stormy Albemarle Sound
the monkey screams all night
and all day from the Chinese Junk
tied up two boats behind us.
A couple visits with cat-groping
kids, gossips about poop they see.
It mounds along the cabin floor
like a mudslide, they tell us.

The monkey begins again.
An aria this time, but
no fat ladies are in sight.
Monster darts out of the V-berth,
eyes glazed, jumps ship,
heads down the path for town.
We all run behind, scream
'Monster! Monster!'.
The monkey sings louder.
Frightened travelers trip
in their haste to escape us.
Monster doubles back,
dives into the boat.
The monkey hits high C.
The cat burrows beneath
the sailbags , remains there,
except at mealtime,
for the next one hundred
nautical miles down
the waterway.

>>Log Entry—
Oct 7-13 Albemarle Sound to Bellhaven

At mile 100 of the Waterway, we meet Albert and Suzanne on the Suzanne in a 20 footer, the first boat we've seen smaller than ours and we decide to travel together for a while. They're a younger couple. Albert has hair down past his shoulders. Suzanne is pretty, doesn't talk much, and is terrified of taking the tiller. They're friendly, but I don't have much in common with either. They started their travels from somewhere within the waterway. Given Suzanne's fears and the not so great condition of their boat, it's a good thing.

We proceed on from the Sound to Bellhaven at mile 137 in freezing rain. Longjohns and winter clothes go on under our wetgear but our noses are frozen by our arrival. We decide to dock for the night to dry things out. Dock fee is $3.50. We pick up shrimp for dinner at $2.20 a pound.

Slower Than A Speeding Bullet

The Waterway grows fat at the Outer Banks.
Land balloons wider, then thins.
The sea seems close enough to touch.
We're slower than a bicyclist,
faster than a walker,
perhaps the speed of a good jogger.
Stinkpotters don't understand
why being a tortoise doesn't bother us.
Most slow when they pass.
Impatient for destination; others roar by,
their wake leaving our boat rocking.
Ahead, Albert pulls out his violin, steers,
foot on the tiller. I'm washing dishes in the cockpit.
A luxury boat idles to our side,
everyone rushing to snap pictures.
I wonder if I'm in someone's photo album already.
How quaint, they may be saying.
I wonder if I was smiling.

>>Log Entry—
Oct 14-17 Bellhaven to Beaufort., North Carolina

Oct 14: *Gale force warnings and cold weather have held us in port so we explore downtown Bellhaven, run into Dave of the Mary Margaret in town in search of a heater for their boat. We're thrilled to find them again, share dinner on their boat and hope to meet up again.*

Oct 15-16: *We cross Pamlico Sound and enter the Neuse River leg of the Waterway, still with Albert and Suzanne. High winds and chop sent us back to harbor on our first attempt to cross Pamlico. At the Neuse River, warnings of storms and gale force winds force us to set out two anchors for the night. We just get them set when black clouds race over the sky and both boats move and strain on their anchor lines. The lines hold, thank goodness. It's still cold and we hope to move further south more quickly.*

Oct 17: *We enter Beaufort, N.C. on a sunny day with dolphins following our boat, see a fawn swimming in the water. We tie up at a city dock under construction and dockage is free until finished. The next day, we row across to picnic on Beaufort's barrier island where shoeless wild ponies still run free. We see tracks in the dunes but not the ponies.*

Storm on the Neuse River

Mother Nature

We fall into the rhythm of sea and sky,
rising at dawn, asleep just after sunset.
The clouds send out long skinny fingers
or bunch up like warm biscuits.
They warn us much better than NOAH
of upcoming squalls or fair weather.
Currents reveal themselves against
the lean of a buoy, a floating leaf;
winds, through the ruff of fur
on a wild goat like the one that glared
from his precarious perch at the Outer Banks.
Dolphins splash around us at Beaufort
and we're danced into the family of sea.

Mother Nature II

The sea gods pick up the pieces of me he shreds,
sing them together so the seams don't split.
I walk the edge of a dream.
Fire burns my hands, my face,
but when I open my eyes
I see it's only the rising moon.

>>Log Entry—
Oct 18-22 Neuse River to Southport, past Cape Fear

Oct 18: *We travel on down the Waterway, then anchor at Wrightsville Beach. Fishermen along the Waterway fill our bucket with extra bluefish they've caught, but our alcohol stove dies that night. The fish sits in the frying pan for almost an hour before the heat is enough to cook it. We row to shore the following day to buy a two-burner Kerosene stove at a marina and are in business again. The Waterway runs swift through here and is shallow. We move to a small park dockage just above Cape Fear.*

Oct 22: *We make our run down the Cape Fear River, current against us, anchoring at Southport, just inside the safety of the Waterway again. Southport is a busy little port and town. We're not here to explore. We replenish our stores and get ready to move on.*

Cape Fear

Lurking in a break-bend in the Waterway
lies Cape Fear River with its seething currents
and forest of strained buoys,
bobbing in frenzied eddies.
Cape Fear, where crazy Robert Mitchum stalked
Gregory Peck to kill him, long before DeNiro
tries the same with Nolte, where stories are told
of boats broaching at the angry mouth
of the inlet if the sea gods were moody that day.
Stomach in knots, I draw, then double-check
course lines from buoy to buoy, my protractor
my salvation, my chart a bible.
The day is a deception in blue and Robert Mitchum,
if he's still around, is hiding.
The boat jerks to the east as the current hits it,
small motor revved up to top speed.
A line of clueless boats follow us
past the ten buoys that twin the one buoy
marking their turn past shoals
and on down the river.
My lover sits quietly with me on this boat,
this brave little boat with its bow held high,
his eyes memorizing the moving water.
I think about the sea miles growing between us.
I try not to think of Robert Mitchum.

>>Log Entry—
Oct24-31 Bucksport S.C. to Charleston

Nov 25-30: We arrange to tie up at Bucksport, S.C. for a week for $9.60 for our trip over to see my parents in Pageland. They pick us and Monster up for the trip. My father's garden is overflowing with fall vegetables so we gather green tomatoes, collards, green peppers and pick up pecans from the back yard. It's strange to be in a house again, to sleep in a bed that doesn't move.

Oct 30-31 : South Santee to Hamlin Creek, just north of Charleston

We dress in Halloween masks Halloween morning, waving at passing boats. By afternoon we have small craft advisories and freezing rain. We set an upended clay flowerpot over our kerosene stove for some heat and to dry out damp socks, keeping the hatch partially open for ventilation. It's barely enough to warm our hands.

All Saints Eve

Cold air has already corralled
us into long johns and jackets
as fall stretches deep
into the Carolinas.
All Saints Eve spirits
are out early today.
They don't want our craft poking
its nose into their mischief, so
summon the wind to discourage us.
Trees curl up their leaves,
bow in homage. Grass flattens
against frightened soil.
A witch criss-crosses the sky.

I look like the lone ranger
in my black eye mask(minus
Tonto and Silver, of course).
He wears a devil's face.

His Jekyll has overcome
Hyde today and I exhale.
When sleet starts we shiver
into raingear, take shorter
turns at the tiller, race ahead
of ghostly companions.
I count down nautical miles
to our next anchorage
where we can hunker into
sleeping bag, bodies warming,
minds blank.

>>Log Entry—
November1-4 Charleston

We find the Mary Margaret docked inside the harbor. We anchor outside. It's a joyful reunion and we decide to travel the rest of the trip into Florida together. The bridge below Charleston has been closed for a week so a lot of boats are holed up waiting to get further south before even worse cold weather hits. We explore Charleston with Dave and Margaret. Despite growing up in the Carolinas, this is my first trip to the city. It's a pleasant surprise. Colorful and pretty. Filled, too, with tourists and a lot of roaming boaters.

Charleston

Shore houses are fitted with Widows Walks,
railed rooftop platforms where women once
watched the heaving horizon for their men to return.
Listen closely and you can still hear a skirt rustle,
the occasional tread of a woman's feet.

The city is a Monet painting.
Flowers are sold on street corners by black women,
hair bound in scarves the color of butterflies.
The old South still folds into itself and endures.

We wander into what we think is a public garden,
sit breathing pink blossoms, legs sprawled.
An elderly man in a blue blazer, dollar bills hovering
in speech bubbles over his head, asks us to leave.
We trudge back onto pastel street in faded jeans,
sailing hats encrusted with sea salt.

By mid-afternoon, we hold hands.
Some days forgiveness comes easier than others.
It drifts in on white magnolia blossoms.

>>Log Entry—
November 4-7 Charleston to Beaufort, S.C.

November 4-5: The bridge opens late afternoon on the 4th so we pass through and anchor fore and aft at the North Edisto River. The current pulls the stern anchor line through R's hands at first attempt so we set another. We've attached water jugs to trip lines to our anchor rodes so we're able to retrieve the lost anchor in the morning light.

Nov 6-7: It's R' s birthday so on the day's run into Beaufort he celebrates by drinking from his gift bottle of scotch beginning that morning. I take the tiller the full day until we reach Beaufort. Neither of us drink when underway so this is unusual. He's in a mood, though. We're in an area of the Waterway where we have to motor, so I don't need his help with the sails. My injured back aches more and more so taking the tiller for the full day is difficult.

We explore the next day, R's temper mollified somewhat. Beaufort is a small town with many beautiful old homes near the water. That night, the Mary Margaret lists to one side at low tide. It turns out that they anchored on a rise of high ground, unmarked on the chart in the anchorage area. Margaret spends the night on Little Adventure while Dave and R attach an anchor to the high side, cranking the line tight to prevent the boat from taking on water as the tide rises again. It's a long night and they re-anchor the following morning.

Birthday Boy

He hauls himself
up from our dinghy
onto cockpit edge
and I know he will
kiss her, if possible.
Suzanne knows, too,
glances at me nervously,
keeps her distance.
It's a stand-off.
High Noon.
But am I John Wayne
or is he?
She's beautiful
toweling her hair,
Beaufort skyline behind her
and I can't blame him.
He goes for his gun.
It's his birthday
and he tries to open-
mouth her. She quickly
moves away. It's clear
that I'm John Wayne
but my pistol is empty.
My theatre audience
yells, leave, Pris, leave.
Meatloaf sings.
I know the movie will end,
just not when.

Why I Stay

Growing up I had to eat vegetables
I disliked in order to get dessert after.
Maybe I generalized incorrectly
from that lesson.

>>Log Entry—
Nov 7 Dave and I plot our next day's run together. It's a become a habit now while Margaret and R make snacks. I comment afterwards that I rarely see other woman do the navigation or take the wheel or tiller for half of the run. Women will take the wheel or tiller while the man uses the head and then again at anchoring time while he drops the anchor. I enjoy both plotting our courses and taking the helm. For me, it's an important part of the trip.

Coming Clean

Marinas worship the stinkpotters.
They guzzle their gas,
plug in every night to run
TV, fridge, A/C or heat.
Sailors can go for a week
on ten bucks of gas, rarely
need power, usually anchor out.
I offer cash for a shower
when we stop for gas.
No's slide down upturned noses.
I could use Aretha's respect song about now.
I'm desperate, want to wash
more than a few square inches
at a time in tiny sink
or bucket poured over my head
in our cockpit.
Their refusal leaves me no choice;
I turn to a life of crime.
Aretha's too late.
Sailing hat on head, bag
slung over one shoulder,
I ask to 'use the facilities'.
Inside, I'm a stripper
in fast forward. Off go the clothes,
out comes shampoo, soap, small
towel and fresh undies.
On comes the warm water.
Wet hair tucked under my sailing hat,
I stroll back to the dock just as gas

and water are paid for.

The One Minute Shower Thief,
my boating friends call me.
So cuff me.

>>Log Entry—

Nov 8 *We anchor in a small creek across from Hilton Head. The currents are very swift, so that we can visit the Mary Margaret only when the current is running our way. They have a motor on their dinghy, so visit us. Dolphins fill the creek. Just as they reach their boat later to board, their dinghy capsizes and the current sweeps them to shore. We hear their voices calling us in the darkness. Fortunately, the current is running that way, so R retrieves them in our dinghy and they haul their now upright dinghy over to their boat. He stays there until tide change and he's able to return. They're okay and Dave is able to clear the dinghy motor of water so that it's fine again, too.*

Sea Children

Dolphins play for an hour in our anchorage
leaping, spinning trails through the purple water.
When late afternoon fishing boats chug
down the waterway for home, nets spread
like giant webs, the dolphins follow.
Across the Waterway, Hilton Head
is a faint glow in the darkness.
The scent of seawater permeates my body.
I become a pillar of salt but, unlike Lot's wife,
it sustains me. I don't crumble.

Dave and Margaret join us for a nightcap.
Margaret and I have drawn close,
almost as close as I am with my siren sisters
still singing out over the white caps
while I travel the narrowing trail of the Waterway.
Margaret is the only one to see my lover's
dark side, through the mirrors he so deftly flashes.
She's my anchor, my eyes when my vision turns cloudy.
We lean back, watch the current rip by.
I think of the dolphins sleeping with one eye open,
brains alert, wonder if they think about us.

>>Log Entry—

Nov 9 We enter Georgia

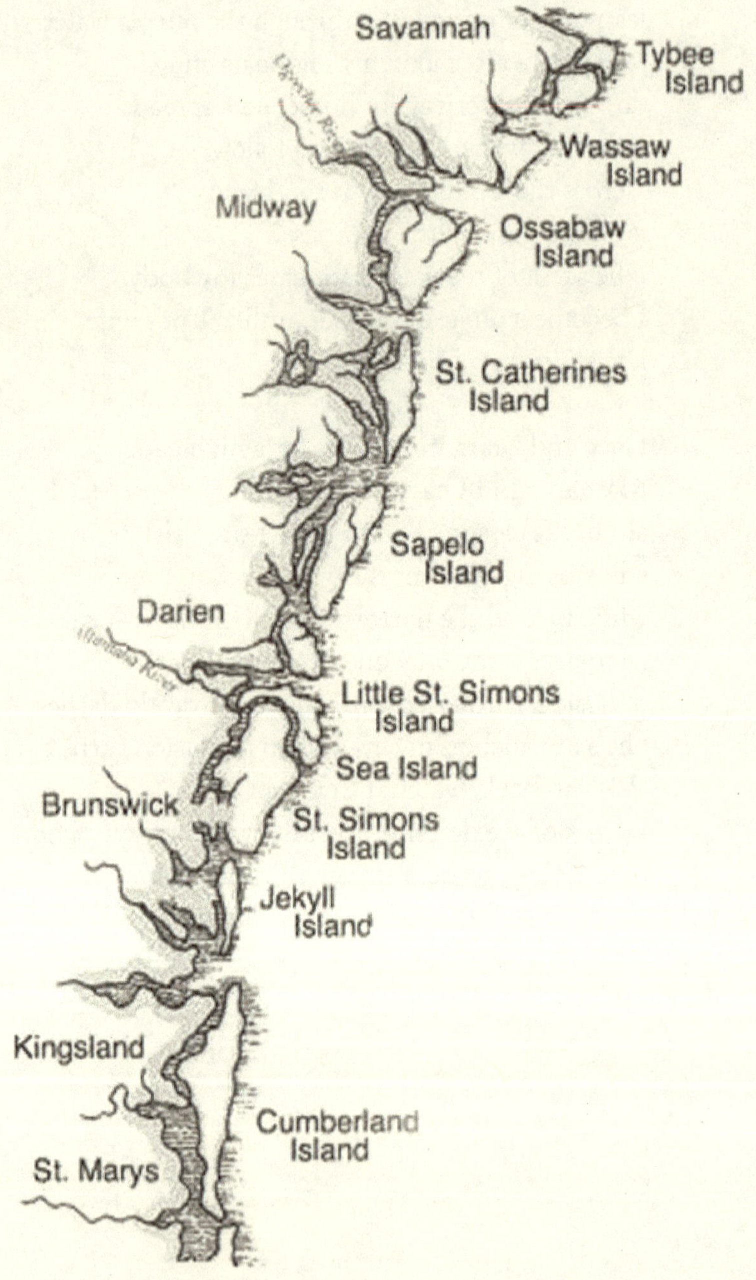

>>Log Entry—
Nov 9-20 Georgia State Line to Florida

Nov 9-11 We anchor off the southernmost of the two Savannah marinas and take the bus in to explore the city two days. It's laid out in town squares much like New England. Downtown is a hilly brick street, filled with art stores and good places to eat.

Riding the Snake

The Waterway becomes a skinny red snake
as it winds near Savannah.
It gobbles red Georgia mud for dinner.
Savannah rises further inland.
It climbs from uneven brick sidewalks
and steep inclines to art shops and classy bars.
A swift moving river borders one edge
but no moat drops for escape.
The squares and old homes remind me of Boston
and I'm momentarily homesick the city
we so casually left behind .
I'm heartsick, too, for days when my lover's face
lit at the sight of me, hands trembling.

Savannah charms with eyes half-lidded,
like a man rising from bed, ready to lure
me back with him if not careful.
Weary of false-hearted Romeos,
I'm ready to ride the snake again.
My feet are restless for moving ground.

>>Log Entry —

Nov12-14 *We enter a very isolated stretch of waterway for three days. Before heading through, a man on a large sailboat in the Savannah marina, his hands in bandages from severe rope burn, asks if we can travel with them. His wife knows nothing about boating and he would like to pay R to drop anchor and haul for him each morning and evening. We agree to travel with him, as well as with the Mary Margaret, but refuse his offer of money. While injured he's been motoring and stopping only at marinas but he doesn't have that option here. I circle each morning and evening until R drops or hauls his anchor, then he comes over and we drop ours. It's easier in strong currents or wind if one person holds the bow up with the engine while the other drops the anchor. We anchor in tiny creeks such as Killenny and Teakettle, then enter civilization again.*

Three days through Georgia

this was how
it once
was
everywhere
no lights
no houses
no towns
no roads
no telephone wires
no marinas
no boom boxes
instead...
trees,
bending over the waterway
the sky,
web-white with stars
silence,
quieter than
a woman's sigh

we almost
relax with each other;
his touch turns tender

such magnificence
can't possibly encircle the soul
and not penetrate

Original Sin

When Adam bedded Eve in these dark pines
I wonder if they laughed in their nakedness,
threw kisses at lopsided stars.
I doubt Adam searched for other Eves to ogle,
found fault or ignored her.
He likely never took joy in jabbing her
with sharp twigs or thorns.
I dream of them cooing blissfully,
serpent and apple still in their future.

Our boat swings with the tide, waking us.
He slides inside. My very own Adam,
already tainted by original sin.

>>Log Entry—
Nov 15-20

We travel with Dave and Margaret on down the state, digging for oysters one evening in an area that's been rating pollution free to eat them. At one point I sink in soft muck to my knees and am afraid I've hit a pocket of quicksand. R is still in the dinghy, holds out an oar and pulls me out. What a relief. We grill the oysters on the Mary Margaret and eat them with homemade noodles in peanut butter sauce, which we made on Little Adventure.

When we reach St Simons Island, we tie up one day to explore the island, itself, then take our boats up the channel and anchor off of Fort Frederica, located on the island. It was one of the largest and most costly forts built by the British in North Carolina. The trees around the fort have thicker trunks than Dave and R put together. After leaving Fort Frederica we travel on to Florida.

Courage

Courage is docking a small boat
with the current shoving your keel
one way, wind pushing your hull
the other and knowing Superman
isn't going to show up to help you.

Sunshine State

We cross the Florida state line
and I expect the sun to turn
into a giant orange, raining juice
into our upturned lips, so cluttered
are the welcome signs, lauding
the glories that are the sunshine state.
Tourists are hi-jacked even on the water
and brochures, free cups of O.J.
are pressed into palms at the
welcome, person-who-may-spend-money dock
just over the state line.
The sultry St Johns River offers
temporary wooded respite but soon
trees are replaced by houses and condos,
staking their own claim by the water.
No deer or wild ponies dare venture
into these Technicolor woods.
Condos shield the wind, so, sails
dropped, we chug along this wet
superhighway for slow travelers.
A half-mile without a house
becomes a miracle, a benediction.
Small planes dragging signs occasionally
fly by. One plane spells out
Eat At Crabby Joe's in cloudy smoke.
My sirens moan in the distance.
They're not welcome here.
Tee's replace sweaters but I'd rather
rewind time, hang an icicle from my nose

I'd rather be charging down the Jersey Coast
again, sirens singing, that angel climbing
over the railing to love me.

>>Log Entry—
Nov 20-24 Thanksgiving

We're across the Florida State line with the Mary Margaret, down through part of the St Johns River, past Jacksonville and Fernandina Beach. We anchor next to Dave and Margaret at St Augustine for Thanksgiving, near the beautiful old bridge across the Waterway. The weather is warmer here but we get rain. We decide to have a special Thanksgiving meal together. We make Peking Duck. All goes well except that the duck catches on fire midway. The fire is put out. The duck is saved. The meal is delicious.

Burned at the Stake

The cabin is gray haze,
sea-soaked towels tossed
over the makeshift oven,
incandescent from flaming grease.
Our poor skewered duck
is bucket dunked, hindquarters
basted black by ash--not molasses.

Disaster is so commonplace
in our boat that sighs of relief
as we finally eat rise giddily
to caress the afternoon sky
and the constant knot
in my chest loosens,
releases in the afterglow.

>>Log Entry—
Nov 26-Nov 29 St Augustine to Daytona

From St Augustine we travel to Daytona Beach, where we see our second movie of the trip, Oh God. The Waterway has changed from an experience in wilderness to a narrow cut of water channeling between condos and expensive homes on each side. I hate it. I like seeing Daytona again, though, close to where I attended college.

Daytona Redux

Me, on this same beach earlier, sandwiched
in time between Blackboard Jungle and the Beatles,
kissing my college boyfriend. Before that,
the jackal lifeguard, baiting his two-roomed trap
with The Four Freshmen, sand beneath bare feet,
hoping to snatch my most sacred possession.
You never forget your first, he whispers.

Time has stood still. The same yellow, pink, blue
two-story motels squat on the shoreline,
garlands for us and the breaking sea.
Cars cuddle near the pier, radios blaring.

The tide pulls back, leaving its stories on shore.
Dave and Margaret, me, him....we walk down
to toe the water.
Four crabs testing the surf.

Dave makes a joke
and laughter cracks my shell open.
Suddenly I know I have what I need without him.
My little boat.
Good friends.
Sea air caressing my face.
This day, so beautiful it could break your heart.

>>Log Entry—
Nov 30-Dec 8 Daytona to Melbourne

Nov 30: We anchor near Merritt Island where Dave and Margaret have friends and we're able to borrow a car. After a visit to Cape Canaveral (now Cape Kennedy), we travel to Melbourne on Dec 2, where Dave and Margaret tentatively plan to relocate after they winter in the Bahamas. Dave hauls their boat and pays R to paint the bottom. We anchor out in the basin to save money and row in. Our money has dwindled and there's enough only for start-up funds someplace new. My back, injured two years ago, has worsened and I can no longer tolerate R's anger. My best choice is to regroup at my parents' home, get help for my back and consider returning to Boston when better, if another job can be found there. R will take the boat on down to West Palm with his brother where his parents have relocated during our trip.

Our journey is suddenly over.

Endings/Beginnings

Money dwindling,
troublesome back inflamed
and fed up,
I pack my duffel
to take flight for
the Carolinas,
my parents' home,
a good doctor.
We'll figure how
to split the boat later.
Our own split takes no
complex calculations.
The dream is over
but I'm not awake yet.
Our mouths meet,
clothes tumbling
around us
for the last time,
moat bridges down,
since we no longer have
castles to protect.
Once again, we become thunder.
Stars form constellations
around our heads.
The wind hums our song.
My heart cracks
into a thousand pieces,
falling as winter rain,
and I don't want to leave

this moment, despite
my cheering fans,
circling birds, clouds
puffing their chests with joy
over our ending.

Home, my first husband calls,
wants me to reread
his letters from Vietnam,
to remember when candles
glimmered briefly at our own feet,
wants to see me.
I say yes, come,
convince myself I still loved him
throughout this insane
addiction to the other,
then *he* calls, hooks me
again with the way
his voice moves
inside, scratching
some lingering need,
the way he tells me
he was a fool, I miss you.
I cancel my first husband's visit.
Yes, come, I stupidly tell him.

Navigation

In a navigational decision
that would have killed me at sea,
I accept his depression explanation,
love protestations,
sudden proposal,
marry him.
He soon sails new waters.
I row in circles,
wander through uncharted territory,
searching for home.

Divorce

Let's just say
he went out
for hamburger
and came home
with a whopper.

While We Were Gone

Elvis Presley dies of a drug induced heart attack.

The first three nodes of the ARPA net are connected in what will eventually become the Internet.

Jimmy Carter, our newly elected President, signs legislation creating the U.S. Department of Energy.

Son of Sam is captured in Yonkers, N.Y.

Voyager 1, then Voyager 2, are launched.

The U.S. agrees to transfer control of The Panama Canal to Panama at the end of the 20th Century.

The last natural smallpox case is discovered in Somalia.

Courageous, skippered by Ted Turner, sweeps Australia to win the 24th America's Cup.

Darth Vader becomes more famous than George Washington.

Aftermath: Thirty Years Later

I remain a child of the sea,
hobbled now with this illness
that netted me, still hear the sirens
calling and so I rise in the night,
thinking to adjust the anchor line,
make sure the boat hasn't slipped.
I rest my hand on the tiller,
watch the stars swell up in greeting,
feel the tide rock the boat again like a cradle.
I'm grateful I didn't wait, didn't
get stuck with only dreams to console me.
The scent of brine fills the room.
A strand of sea grass appears in my hand.
My sirens' parting gift before daybreak.

Afterword

R and I married in early 1978. We sold Little Adventure for down payment on a house. He left unexpectedly Thanksgiving of 1979 and remarried six months later. Our divorce was final in February 1980. The second goodbye was painful, but, hindsight, it was the best thing that could've happened to me. My decision to overlook past problems and marry R. was probably among the worst decisions I'd made. We made one last attempt to patch things but it only prolonged the inevitable. If I had the choice to make over again about the trip, however, I would do the same thing. The joy of traveling by sea transcended the relationship issues. It became a song I still sing. It reshaped my perception of what's important in life.

I remarried a year after the divorce and am still married to the same man. In 1988 my husband and I took our 26 foot sailboat across to the Bahamas for a vacation, sailing down the Abacos as far as Green Turtle Cay. R and I had originally planned to extend our trip this far, possibly further. I managed to make this leg of the trip, after all, even if over ten years later and with a different man.

That gives me a sense of closure, a feeling of satisfaction.

About the Author

The poetry of Pris Campbell has appeared in such journals as *Chiron Review, Boxcar Poetry Review, Main Street Rag, OCHO*, and *Wild Goose Review*. She was featured poet in 2008/2009 in *Empowerment4Women, In the Fray,* and *From East to West*. In 2008, she was nominated for a Pushcart Prize. Her most recent chapbook, *Hesitant Commitments,* was published by LUMMOX Press (www.lummoxpress.com) and is part of the Little Red Book series. Before she was sidelined by CFIDS in 1990, Pris was a Clinical Psychologist, working in St Louis, Honolulu, Providence, and Boston, ending up in the greater West Palm Beach, FL, where she currently lives with her husband, a sea loving dog and a cat who sleeps on her poetry drafts.

Cover Photos: *Little Adventure* anchored at Hull, MA; Pris Campbell exiting the East River, entering New York Harbor.

ABOUT THE LUMMOX PRESS

Lummox Press was created in 1994 by RD Armstrong. It began as a self-publishing/DIY imprint for poetry by RD. Several chapbooks were published and in late 1995 it began publishing the **Lummox Journal**, a monthly small/underground press lit-arts zine. Available primarily by subscription, the LJ continued it's exploration of the "creative process" until its demise as a print mag in 2006.

During its eleven year existence, this tiny mag with the big name, interviewed poets, musicians and artists (over 100 in all) about how they do what they do. Hundreds of poems were also published in its pages. Poets like ***Todd Moore, Lyn Lifshin, Gerald Locklin, Holly Prado, L.A. Bogen, Linda Lerner, Scott Wannberg, Philomene Long, John Thomas*** and ***RD Armstrong,*** to name a few, appeared regularly within its pages. It was hailed as one of the best monthly's in the small press.

In 1998, Lummox began publishing the **Little Red Book** series, and continues to do so today. To date there are some 63 titles in the series (as of 2009) and this year a collection of poems from the first decade of the series has been published under the title, **The Long Way Home** (2009).

Lummox also publishes limited edition books

such as **The Wren Notebook** by Rick Smith (2000) and **Last Call: The Legacy of Charles Bukowski** (2004). More recently, Lummox published a set of four titles from its founder, RD Armstrong: **On/Off the Beaten Path** (a trio of long poems about road trips taken in 1999, 2000 and 2001 including the epic poem **RoadKill** – which John Berbrich said was "the best post 9-11 writing I've seen"), **Fire and Rain – Selected Poems 1993-2007 Volumes 1 & 2** and **El Pagano and Other Twisted Tales** (a collection of short stories and flash fiction). All were published in 2008. In late 2008 Lummox began publishing the ***RESPECT*** series starting with ***John Yamrus'*** **New and Selected Poems.** This was followed by ***Todd Moore's*** **The Riddle of the Wooden Gun** (2009); **Sea Trails** by ***Pris Campbell*** (2009) and **Down This Crooked Road – Modern Poetry from the Road Less Traveled** edited by ***RD Armstrong and William Taylor, Jr.*** (2009). These books are available directly from the Lummox Press via the website: www.lummoxpress.com or at **Lummox** c/o PO Box 5301 San Pedro, CA 90733. There are also E-Book versions of most titles available. The RESPECT series, as well as, RD's four titles are also available at Amazon.com.

Please visit the website to read selections from these titles as well as peruse the many other titles/articles published by the Lummox Press.

Ask your independent bookstore to carry these titles, since Lummox only deals with independent book stores like Powell's of Portland, OR; The Book Collector of Sacramento, CA or Moe's of Berkeley, CA.

Together with Chris Yeseta (Layout and Art Direction since 1997), RD continues to publish books that are both striking in their looks as well as their content...you'd think he was aping Black Sparrow, but he is merely trying to produce the best books he can for his clients, the poets, and their customers, you, the readers.

* * *

ABOUT RAINDOG

RD Armstrong (Raindog to his friends) lives in Long Beach, CA and plies his trade as a HANDY-MAN & journeyman POET all over the Southern California area.

RD has been writing and actively participating in the poetry "scene" in the Los Angeles area for fifteen years. During his travels, he has met and befriended many Small Press poets, and can count among these both the famous and infamous. He divides his time between operating the Lummox Press, publishing the Little Red Book &

the new RESPECT series, writing and working on the houses of his customers. What started out as his avocation, writing poetry and fiction, has now taken a back seat to his obligations as a small press mogul! Poetry has become a closeted obsession.

ABOUT THE NAME RAINDOG – it comes from a song/album by Tom Waits. It describes a dog that has lost his way in this crazy world.

CONTACT:
poetraindog@gmail.com
www.lummoxpress.com

www.ingramcontent.com/pod-product-compliance
Lightning Source LLC
LaVergne TN
LVHW050936080826
845145LV00004B/1279

* 9 7 8 1 9 2 9 8 7 8 0 2 4 *